STUNNING
GARNISHES

Consulting Editor:
Valerie Ferguson

southwater

Contents

Introduction 4

Equipment 6

Useful Staples 8

Easy Ways with Herbs 10

Simple Vegetable Garnishes 12

Using Fruit and Flowers 14

Basic Techniques 16

Simple Garnishes 20

Sensational Garnishes 30

Special Occasions 50

Introduction

Many factors contribute to our enjoyment of the food we eat, and one of the most important is its appearance. A dish that is attractively presented whets the appetite. Even the simplest garnish—a slice of lemon or sprig of parsley—adds an appealing finishing touch. A more elaborate or unusual garnish—gilded fruit or edible flowers—intrigues and delights.

This book is packed with ideas for garnishing every course, from soup to dessert. There are quick and easy garnishes for informal meals and family suppers, using inexpensive herbs, fruits and vegetables. More spectacular garnishes are appropriate for dinner parties and special occasions, and there are sensational suggestions using a wide range of ingredients, from avocados to chocolate and from pastry to rose petals.

Where a garnish is intended to decorate an individual plate, the recipe is for a single serving. Garnishes for serving platters are marked as such. All are easily adapted for the number of servings needed.

Whether you are planning a romantic meal for two, a dinner party or a celebratory buffet, include the final flourish of the perfect garnish.

Equipment

It is not necessary to have elaborate gadgets for making garnishes, but a few specialty items make the task easier.

Cannelle Knife

This is useful for carving stripes in the zest of citrus fruits and for decorating soft-skinned vegetables, such as cucumbers. Pare off thin strips before slicing to make a decorative edge.

Cutters

Round, square and other shapes of cutters, such as hearts and stars, can be used to stamp out shapes from thinly sliced vegetables and fruits, and citrus peel. Tiny cutters are available in a variety of shapes.

Knives

A small turning, or paring, knife is essential for carving designs on vegetables, such as radishes, and for fluting mushrooms. A sharp cook's knife or chopping knife has a multitude of uses.

Melon Baller

This useful tool is available with large and small scoops.

Mezzaluna

Used for finely chopping herbs and vegetables. A larger size is suitable for all purposes.

Pastry Brushes

Good-quality brushes with tightly packed bristles are best.

Piping Bags and Nozzles

A medium bag with a selection of nozzles can be used for garnishing both sweet and savory dishes. Use small disposable piping bags for chocolate when a fine line is needed.

Raffia

Available in a range of colors, this is much more attractive than string for tying small bunches of herbs or flowers and can be bought at most florists or garden centers.

Ribbon

Keep a small stock in various colors and widths for tying around cold soufflés and securing bunches of herbs or posies of fresh flowers.

Sieves

Both large and small sieves are essential kitchen tools. Simply dusting a cake with sifted confectioners' sugar can make an attractive finish.

Skewers and Toothpicks

These are useful for a variety of purposes, such as teasing out the leaves in herb bouquets or dragging a spot of cream through a fruit sauce to make a marbled or feathered pattern.

Small Scissors

These are ideal for small garnishes and when knives would be difficult to use. They are also useful for snipping chives and other herbs.

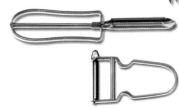

Swivel-blade Vegetable Peelers

Both long-handled and broad-handled peelers are good for paring vegetables into thin strips, paring peel from citrus fruits and shaving cheese, as well as peeling vegetables.

Tea Strainer

This is the right size for sifting confectioners' sugar or cocoa powder onto individual mousses and single servings of desserts.

Zester

Useful for making strips in citrus zest and cucumbers, this is similar to a cannelle knife, but produces a row of thin stripes.

Useful Staples

Keep these items handy in the kitchen and you will never have a problem making an instant garnish. Many can be made in advance and stored for later use.

Cookies and Crackers

Make a supply of cookies and crackers. Cut them into decorative shapes, bake and then store in an airtight container or freeze. Thaw for 30 minutes before using.

Chocolate

Semi-sweet, milk and white chocolate are useful for decorating cakes and desserts. Chocolate curls can be made up to a month in advance and stored on waxed paper in an airtight container in a cool place.

Cinnamon Sticks

Tie bundles of long cinnamon sticks together with ribbon or raffia and store in an airtight container. Place them at the side of serving plates for an unusual touch.

Cucumbers

Keep a cucumber in the refrigerator for a variety of garnishes.

Dried Chiles

Large and small dried chiles look stunning in a bowl in the kitchen and are great as a garnish when tied together with raffia.

Fresh Chiles

Bright red and green chiles make an attractive addition to spicy dishes. Tie in small bunches with raffia, adding one or two sprigs of fresh herbs, if desired.

Fruit Purées

Made in advance and frozen in ice cube trays, these are great for decorating desserts. Thaw in the microwave or in a saucepan, swirl on a plate and top with the dessert.

Herb Butter

Rolls of herb butter can be frozen, ready for slicing at a moment's notice. Serve on top of meat, poultry or fish.

Herbs

The best herbs are home-grown, but purchased herbs will stay fresh in the refrigerator for 4–5 days. Trim the ends, wash and shake well, then place on damp paper towels in a storage box.

Lemons and Limes

These fruits keep well and are useful for both sweet and savory dishes.

Oranges

Unpeeled oranges can be cut into wedges or slices, and slices can be turned into cones or twists.

Parmesan Cheese

Keep in a single piece in the refrigerator and use freshly shaven curls for garnishing pasta and salads.

Above: Attractive garnishes can be made using the simplest, readily available ingredients.

Radishes

Left whole, with their leaves attached, radishes are perfect for garnishing salads or plates of sandwiches. Carved into roses and other patterns, they make more elegant garnishes.

Red Currants

Bunches of red currants tied with chives make a stunning and unusual garnish for savory dishes. Small bunches of fruit look attractive draped on desserts.

Easy Ways with Herbs

Fresh herbs are wonderfully versatile. They can be chopped, sliced, used in strands or bound in a bouquet.

Basil
A cluster of leaves looks great with tomatoes. Sprinkle single leaves on salads and pizzas to add to the flavor and appearance.

Bay
Use the glossy leaves singly or in small sprigs to garnish roast meat and poultry and any recipe that includes bay. As an evergreen, bay is available all year round.

Carrot Tops
Not strictly an herb, but young feathery carrot tops make an unusual garnish for platters, simply laid alongside the prepared food.

Chives
These can be prepared in a variety of ways: finely snipped or chopped, coarsely chopped, cut on the diagonal or wilted and braided or tied.

Cilantro
Fresh sprigs are essential for garnishing Asian dishes, and the chopped herb can be sprinkled on all sorts of savory Indian dishes.

Dill
This looks great snipped into fronds or finely chopped and sprinkled on food. Use sprigs of fresh dill with a twist of lemon to garnish fish dishes.

Fennel

The delicate green fronds look similar to dill and can be used in the same way. Fennel, with its aniseed flavor, is particularly suited to fish and Mediterranean-style dishes.

Mixed Herbs

All herbs look good just poking out from beneath a simple lemon or cucumber slice or twist. Form small bunches of herbs in a bouquet and tie with raffia or a wilted chive. Twist off the stems and tease out the leaves with a toothpick.

Parsley

A traditional garnish for fish and soups, parsley can be used for many other dishes too. Use whole small sprigs of flat-leaf parsley to garnish individual plates. Finely chop curly parsley and sprinkle on rice, potatoes, puréed vegetables and other dishes to add color and a delicate fresh herb flavor.

Sage

Add this pungent herb to bouquets for color and texture and use on its own to garnish pork dishes. Purple or tricolor sages are particularly stunning and can be used to great effect.

Scented Geranium

The finely-serrated leaves make an attractive decoration for ice creams and sorbets. As well as the plain green variety, there is also an interesting variegated type. Use the whole leaves in place of mint sprigs for an unusual bouquet.

Watercress

A simple garnish of watercress can brighten a plate of sandwiches, or fish, poultry and beef dishes, with its deep green color and fresh appearance. Gather several sprigs, twist off the ends of the stems and place on the side of serving platters, or use a single sprig on smaller individual plates.

Simple Vegetable Garnishes

In addition to the ever-popular and versatile cucumber, a variety of vegetables can be chopped and sliced to make colorful garnishes.

Carrot Bundles

Blanch a long chive in a small pan of boiling water for 20–30 seconds.

Carrot Bundle

Drain, refresh in cold water, then drain and dry. Cut eight carrot matchsticks 2 inches long. Use the wilted chive to tie the matchsticks into a neat bundle.

Carrot Matchsticks

Peeled carrots can be cut into 2-inch lengths, then thinly sliced. Stack the slices, then cut into thin matchsticks.

Cucumber

The most widely used vegetable garnish, cucumber can be prepared in a variety of ways.

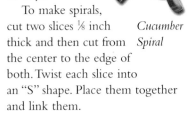

Cucumber Spiral

To make spirals, cut two slices ⅛ inch thick and then cut from the center to the edge of both. Twist each slice into an "S" shape. Place them together and link them.

To make a border, cut six slices ⅛ inch thick, then cut each slice in half. Place around the rim of the plate, alternating the way they face.

To make a fan, cut a 2-inch piece of cucumber in half lengthwise. Make six or seven very fine cuts three-quarters of the way into the half. Press down gently and fan out the slices.

Cucumber Border

Cucumber Fan

Green Beans

Slice at an angle into ¾-inch lengths. Sprinkle on salads or use in pairs to make crosses on top of a canapé.

Green Beans

Leek Curls

Cut a leek into 2-inch lengths, then slice in half lengthwise. Cut the slices into fine matchsticks. Put them in a bowl of ice water and chill for 2 hours, until they form tight curls. Drain before using.

Leek Curls

Mushrooms

Use a small sharp knife to cut small grooves in a spiral in the caps of button mushrooms. Use raw or lightly sautéed in butter.

Bell Pepper Triangles

Bell Pepper Triangles

Seed and core a red and a yellow pepper. Cut out ¾ x ½-inch rectangles. Make a cut two-thirds of the way into the short side, three-quarters of the way up. Turn the pepper 180° and repeat. Twist the pepper and pull to form a triangle. Alternate red and yellow triangles around the rim of a plate as a border, or use just one or two as a garnish for individual servings.

Radishes

Make even zigzag cuts around the middle and pull apart to make Vandyke radishes.

Vandyke Radish

Scallions

Use a sharp knife to cut the green ends into shreds, leaving them still attached to the white part. Put them in a bowl of ice water and chill for at lest 4 hours, until the ends curl. This can also be done with shorter lengths of shredded scallion. Sprinkle them on salads and hot savory dishes.

Tomato

Using a small, sharp knife, cut a "V" into the middle of a large, firm tomato, inserting the knife through to the center. Make identical cuts all around the tomato to create a zigzag line. Gently pull the tomato apart and top each half with two quarter slices of cucumber and a parsley sprig.

Tomato Rose

13

Using Fruit and Flowers

Some of the most eye-catching garnishes and decorations are made from simply cut and arranged fruit and flowers.

Baby Rose Posy

Trim the stems of six perfect small roses to about 1 inch. Place five of the roses in a ring on a cake so that the stems meet in the center. Place the remaining rose on top to finish the posy.

Baby Rose Posy

Edible Flowers

Use edible flowers, such as nasturtiums or chives, to enliven a salad, or use sweet violets or lavender with a scoop of ice cream. Both blue and white borage flowers look stunning in salads and drinks during the summer months. Other edible flowers include primroses, pansies, mallow, calendula marigolds and elder.

Edible Flowers

Flower Bouquet

Gather some fresh flowers together in a bouquet and tie with raffia or a ribbon and place on top of a cake just before serving.

Flower Bouquet

Lemon Basket

Holding a lemon lengthwise, cut it in half around the middle to within ¼ inch of the center. Make an identical cut on the opposite side of the lemon. Slice down from the top to meet the first incision, then make a similar cut from the top to meet the second. Pull out the loose segments and discard, or use for another purpose. Cut out the flesh from under the "handle" and discard. Put a sprig of dill in the center of the lemon basket and place on a dish of canapés or use to garnish a large whole cooked fish.

Lemon Basket

Lemon and Lime Wedges

Cut a lemon or lime in half lengthwise, then cut each half into three wedges. Remove any seeds. Arrange the wedges on the plate in pairs, separated by a sprig of parsley.

Lemon Wedges

Melon Bowl

Insert a small, sharp knife halfway through a cantaloupe at an angle, and push it in as far as the center. Cut a series of deep "V" shapes all the way around the melon. Gently pull the melon apart and remove the seeds. Using a melon baller, scoop the flesh of one half into small balls and place these in the cavity of the other half.

Melon Bowl

Orange Flower

Using a sharp knife, cut two thin slices from an orange, then cut each slice in half. Cut along the inside of the pith on one half to within ⅛ inch of the end. Turn the strip of zest

Orange Flower

in to form a loop on top of the half slice. Repeat with the remaining half slices. Place them in a ring with the loops on the outside.

Pear Fan

Peel a fairly firm pear, leaving the stem intact. Poach in a light syrup until tender. Cut the poached pear in half lengthwise. Place the pear cut-side down on a cutting board and cut about eight thin slices, leaving them intact at the top. Press down gently to fan the slices.

Pear Fan

Strawberry Fan

Cut a firm, ripe strawberry into thin slices from the pointed end almost to the top. Leave the hull and calyx in place to add color contrast, and gently fan out the slices. Make half fans by halving the strawberry first. Place cut-side down on a cutting board and make cuts from the leaf end almost to the pointed end and fan out gently.

Strawberry Fan

Using a Cannelle Knife

Create a decorative effect by carving stripes in citrus zest or cucumber peel.

1 Holding the fruit or vegetable in one hand, pull the cannelle knife along the surface at regular intervals to carve grooves in the zest or skin.

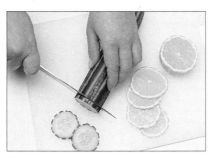

2 Using a sharp knife, cut the fruit or vegetable horizontally to make pretty, ridged slices.

VARIATION: If preferred, use the grooved fruit and vegetables to make spirals, fans or decorated wedges.

Chopping Herbs with a Mezzaluna

Using this tool with a two-handled, curved blade is the easiest and safest way to chop herbs.

1 Pull the leaves off the stems with your fingers until they are stripped. Place the leaves in a pile on a cutting board.

2 Chop by rocking the mezzaluna from side to side, like a seesaw, over the herb leaves until they are as coarse or fine as desired.

Julienne Strips using a Peeler and Knife

The zest of oranges, lemons or limes can be sprinkled on hot or cold desserts for an easy decoration.

1 Using a swivel-blade vegetable peeler, pare thin strips of colored zest from the citrus fruit, avoiding the white pith underneath.

2 Stack the pieces of zest and use a sharp knife to cut into very thin shreds. Use immediately or blanch briefly in boiling water, refresh in cold water and dry well on paper towels.

Julienne Strips using a Zester

The colorful zest of citrus fruits is full of flavor, but the pith is bitter, so it is important not to include it.

1 Choose unwaxed citrus fruit, if possible. It is a wise precaution to wash and dry the fruit in any case.

2 Holding the fruit firmly on a cutting board with one hand, draw a citrus zester across the zest to remove fine strips. Avoid the pith just underneath the skin.

Blanching

Vegetables, fruits or herbs can be briefly immersed in boiling water to make them more pliable and easier to handle.

1 Fill a large saucepan with water and bring to a boil. Add the prepared vegetable, fruit or herb for the time specified in the recipe—usually 1–2 minutes.

2 Drain well in a colander, then refresh in cold water. Change the water once or twice, as necessary, until the food is completely cold. Drain well and pat dry.

COOK'S TIP: Blanched fruits and vegetables can be cut into diamonds.

Peeling Tomatoes

It takes only minutes to peel tomatoes, but it makes all the difference to the dish.

1 Make a small cross in the skin on the base of each tomato. Cut out the calyx with a small, sharp knife.

2 Place the tomatoes in boiling water for 20–30 seconds, drain and refresh under cold water. Gently peel off the loosened skin.

COOK'S TIP: The peeled tomatoes can be quartered, then the seeds and core can be removed. The flesh can then be cut into small squares.

Marbling and Feathering

This is a simple but effective technique for decorating sauces and soups.

1 For marbling, flood a plate with dark-colored sauce, then trickle on a little cream. Drag the cream through the sauce with the point of a fine metal skewer or toothpick, swirling it to achieve a marble effect.

2 For feathering, flood a plate with dark-colored sauce. Fill a piping bag, fitted with a small nozzle, with cream. Pipe dots of cream around the edge. Drag the cream through the sauce with the point of a fine metal skewer or toothpick to form "tails."

Stenciling

This is a quick and easy way to liven up sponge cakes, cookies and cold soufflés. You could experiment with different templates, such as paper doilies.

1 Place a cake on a sheet of waxed paper. Cut out strips of paper and lay these in a random, criss-cross pattern across the top of the cake. Dust with sifted confectioners' sugar, then carefully remove the paper strips to reveal the pattern.

2 For a two-tone effect, dust a cake with sifted confectioners' sugar, covering it completely. Place a doily lightly over the cake and dust with sifted cocoa powder. Lift off carefully.

Herb-rimmed Plate

Try garnishing the rim of the plate rather than the food itself—a very simple but eye-catching idea.

FOR THE GARNISH
1 tablespoon butter, softened
2 tablespoons chopped fresh chives

1 Brush the butter around the rim of the plate. Sprinkle the chives on the butter to form a decorative edge. Tilt the plate and shake gently to remove any loose chives. Use the plate for serving canapés or finger foods at a buffet or to decorate a seafood salad for a dinner party.

Herb Bouquet

Mixed herbs, tied together attractively, are the perfect garnish for grilled whole fish, steak, chops or terrines.

FOR THE GARNISH
½ bunch mixed fresh herbs, such as parsley, chives, dill and rosemary
raffia, for tying

1 Starting with several long-stemmed pieces of parsley, make a bouquet, adding chives, dill and rosemary or other herbs of your choice. Herbs in flower are particularly attractive; use stems of different lengths.

2 Tie a long piece of raffia around the bouquet, about three-quarters of the way down. Wind the raffia around several times to make a wide band and finish with a knot or large bow. Cut the herb stems level and trim the raffia ends at an angle. Arrange the bouquet at an angle on whole fish or plain grilled meat.

Parmesan Curls

Several perfectly formed curls of Parmesan cheese give a simple plate of pasta a real lift.

FOR THE GARNISH
1 piece of Parmesan cheese

1 It is wise to make the Parmesan curls before cooking the pasta unless you are very practiced. Holding a swivel-blade vegetable peeler at an angle of 45°, draw it firmly and steadily across the Parmesan cheese to form a curl. Make three to four curls for each serving. Cover lightly and set aside until ready to serve.

Vegetable Shreds

These strips of colorful vegetables look wonderful with crêpes and blinis and are perfect for garnishing chicken and fish.

FOR THE GARNISH
¼ red bell pepper, seeded
¼ yellow bell pepper, seeded
¼ green bell pepper, seeded
½ small carrot, peeled
¼ cucumber

1 Using a sharp knife, cut the peppers, carrot and cucumber into julienne strips about ¾ inch long and ¼ inch wide. Transfer to a plate, cover with plastic wrap and chill in the refrigerator until needed.

2 When serving, divide the vegetable strips among the food or individual plates and either arrange them to form little multicolored "haystacks" or sprinkle them randomly.

Chive Flowers

The simplest dishes—from scrambled eggs to sandwiches—become something special when garnished with chive flowers.

FOR THE GARNISH
1 tablespoon chive flowers
snipped chives

1 Cut the chive flower-heads from the main stem, then snip off each floret, removing as much of the little stems as possible.

2 Sprinkle the florets on the dish to make a garland, or arrange one or two in a decorative pattern with the chives.

Orange Segments

Not just for desserts, orange or lemon segments make an appealing garnish for fish, poultry and salads.

FOR THE GARNISH
1 orange

1 Peel the orange with a small, sharp knife, removing all the peel, including the white pith and outer membrane.

2 Holding the peeled orange over a bowl to catch the juice, run a knife down each side of the membrane between each segment and remove the segments cleanly.

Red Bell Pepper Bundles

A colorful garnish for fish steaks, grilled meats and shellfish.

FOR THE GARNISH
2 long chives
¼ red bell pepper, seeded

1 Blanch the chives in a small pan of boiling water for 20–30 seconds, until just wilted. Drain, refresh in cold water and drain again. With a sharp knife, cut the pepper into matchsticks.

2 Tie the pepper strips together in bundles of 8–10 with a chive. Arrange on the side of a serving dish.

Asparagus Bundles

Fine asparagus spears look elegant gathered in a bundle.

FOR THE GARNISH
3 slender asparagus spears
1 long green scallion stem
salt

1 Cook the asparagus in lightly salted boiling water for about 8 minutes or until tender, then drain. Blanch the scallion stem in a small pan of boiling water for 20–30 seconds, until just wilted. Drain, refresh in cold water and drain again.

2 Place the asparagus spears together, staggering the tips ¾ inch below each other. Tie them together with the wilted scallion stem. Trim the base of the bundle of asparagus at an angle and trim the end of the scallion tie. Use the asparagus bundle to garnish risotto, chicken, ham or omelet.

Chile Bouquets

Chiles make a bright garnish to set off a plate.

FOR THE GARNISH
2 large fresh red chiles
raffia, for tying
large sprigs of fresh parsley or
    cilantro (optional)

1 Tie the stems of the chiles together with a small piece of raffia. For an interesting contrast, add a large sprig of fresh parsley or cilantro.

2 Use to garnish a platter of vegetables, cold meats, kebabs, quiche or canapés.

Radish Roses

This classic garnish is actually quite easy to make and looks superb on a platter of cold meats or seafood.

FOR THE GARNISH
radishes
ice water

1 Working on one radish at a time, remove the stem and, with the pointed end of a vegetable knife, cut petal shapes around the bottom half of the radish, keeping them joined at the base.

2 Using the vegetable knife, cut a second row of petals of equal size in between and above the first row. Continue in this way until you reach the top of the radish.

3 Place the radish roses in a bowl of ice water in the refrigerator for at least 1 hour, until opened out. Drain well and use the roses to garnish cold platters, sandwiches and canapés.

Lemon Leaves

Lemon is the classic garnish for fish dishes, but these pretty leaves can be used for other dishes too.

FOR THE GARNISH
1 unwaxed lemon

1 Cut a small "V" from the side of the lemon. Repeat at ¼-inch intervals. Use to garnish fish dishes, terrines, caviar and smoked salmon as well as salads and poultry dishes.

VARIATION: Other citrus fruit suitable for this kind of garnish are grapefruit, blood oranges and limes.

Lime Twists

Brightly colored, these twists will enliven kebabs and other grilled dishes such as fish, meat and poultry.

FOR THE GARNISH
1 lime
4–6 sprigs of cilantro

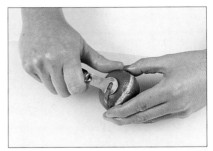

1 Using a cannelle knife, cut stripes lengthwise down the zest of the lime at ½-inch intervals. Cut the lime into ¼-inch slices.

2 Make a cut from the center to the edge of each lime slice and then twist into an "S" shape. Top each twist with a sprig of cilantro and arrange around a serving platter.

Herbed Lime Wedges

Limes are wonderfully versatile and look great cut into wedges, then dusted with chopped herbs.

FOR THE GARNISH
1 lime
½ cup cilantro or parsley

1 Cut the lime in half lengthwise and then cut the halves into wedges. Finely chop the cilantro or parsley.

2 Press the long edge of each lime wedge into the chopped herb. Arrange the wedges on a serving plate to garnish fish, seafood or pâté.

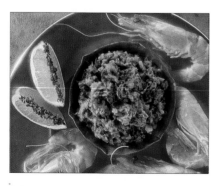

Lemon Spirals

Linking several lemon twists together with a sprig of parsley creates a simple but effective result.

FOR THE GARNISH
1 lemon
sprigs of fresh parsley

1 Using a sharp knife, cut the lemon into ¼-inch slices. Make a cut in each slice starting from the center out to the skin.

2 Hold the slice either side of the cut and twist to form an "S" shape. Place three together to form a spiral. Add a sprig of parsley. Use to garnish smoked fish pâté or kebabs.

Chile Flowers

These delicate flowers need plenty of time to open fully.

FOR THE GARNISH
6 fresh red or green chiles
ice water

1 Using a small pair of scissors or a slim-bladed knife, carefully cut each chile lengthwise up from the tip to within ½ inch of the stem end. Repeat this at regular intervals around the chiles.

2 Rinse the chiles in cold water and remove all the seeds. Place the chiles in a bowl of ice water and chill for at least 4 hours.

Red Currant Bunches

These colorful berries tied with chives are the perfect garnish for roast lamb or lamb chops.

FOR THE GARNISH
1 chive
2 small bunches red currants

1 Blanch the chive in boiling water for 20–30 seconds, until just wilted. Drain, refresh in cold water and drain again.

2 Tie the bunches of red currants together by wrapping the chive around the stems. Tie neatly and trim the ends. Use to garnish lamb, turkey or venison.

Radish Dahlias

This garnish looks most effective when prepared with deep-red globe radishes.

FOR THE GARNISH
radishes
ice water

1 Working on one radish at a time, remove the stem. Using a sharp knife, cut downward across the radish at ⅛-inch intervals, keeping the radish joined at the base. Then cut in the opposite direction to form minute squares.

2 Place the radishes in a bowl of ice water and chill for at least 1 hour, until the petals open out. Drain and use to garnish cold platters, salads, sandwiches and canapés.

Scallion Diagonals and Shreds

Use scallions to garnish soups, fish, seafood and rice dishes.

FOR THE GARNISH
1 bunch scallions, trimmed

1 For diagonals, thickly slice the scallions, holding the knife at an angle of about 60°.

2 For shreds, cut the scallions into 2-inch lengths, slice each piece in half lengthwise, then into fine shreds.

Quick Chocolate Scrolls

Choose semi-sweet, milk or white chocolate to decorate trifles, mousses and other creamy desserts.

FOR THE GARNISH
2 ounces chocolate, at room temperature

1 Use a swivel blade vegetable peeler to shave scrolls of chocolate from the side of the bar.

COOK'S TIP: For wider scrolls, use a thicker bar of chocolate.

Mango Fan

Mangoes have a wonderful texture and look superb simply fanned out to decorate fruit desserts and tarts.

FOR THE GARNISH
1 mango
confectioners' sugar, for dusting

1 Using a sharp knife, slice the flesh off both sides of the mango pit and cut each piece in half lengthwise. Make five cuts, almost to the end, in each quarter.

2 Dust the sliced mango with confectioners' sugar. Transfer the mango quarters to a serving dish and gently spread out the slices into a fan.

Chive Braids

These eye-catching braids look wonderful floating on the surface of a bowl of creamy soup.

FOR THE GARNISH
10 thick chives, about 8 inches long

1 Pick out three of the thickest chives and two that are thinner. Align the thicker chives on a work surface with a bowl or board on one end to hold them still. Braid the chives together to within 1 inch of the end.

2 Tie one of the thinner chives around the exposed end of the braid. Remove the bowl or board and tie the other end the same way. Trim the ends of the braids and tie neatly with kitchen scissors. Make a second braid in the same way.

3 Place the braids in a bowl and pour boiling water on them. Let stand for 20–30 seconds, then drain and refresh under cold water. Drain again.

COOK'S TIP: Use chive braids to tie small bunches of herbs for garnishing flans, seafood or salads.

Avocado Fan

With their pale green flesh, avocados undoubtedly are one of the most elegant and sophisticated garnishes.

FOR THE GARNISH
1 avocado

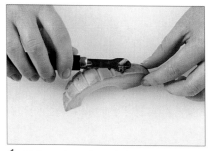

2 Make four cuts lengthwise down each avocado quarter, leaving ½ inch intact at the end. Carefully fan out the avocado slices, by pressing gently with your fingers, and arrange them on individual serving plates to garnish salads, or use on a platter of cold meats or shellfish.

1 Halve, pit and peel the avocado. Slice each half lengthwise into quarters. Gently draw a cannelle knife across the quarters at ½-inch intervals to create regular stripes.

Scallion Brushes

A traditional garnish for Chinese food, scallion brushes are equally effective on many Western dishes.

FOR THE GARNISH
8 scallions
ice water

1 Trim the scallions, removing the roots and bulbs. Cut off the tops at an angle to give a total length of about 6 inches.

2 Using a fine-bladed knife, make 2-inch lengthwise cuts in the white part of each scallion. Keep the cuts parallel and as close together as possible. Place the scallions in a bowl of ice water and chill for at least 4 hours, until curled. Drain.

COOK'S TIP: Prepared in this way, scallions are perfect for brushing a marinade on grilled food. They can also be served with crispy duck and Chinese pancakes and used to dip in the hoisin sauce.

Tomato Finger Fans

This colorful and unusual garnish is perfect for terrines and pâtés and looks great with finger foods on a buffet table.

FOR THE GARNISH
3–4 firm tomatoes
sprigs of fresh flat-leaf parsley

1 Cut the tomatoes into quarters. Hold each quarter skin-side down and use the knife to scoop out the pulp and seeds.

2 Make four cuts down the length of each tomato quarter, leaving about ½ inch intact at the top. Turn the tomato quarter over and carefully fan out with the fingers. Top each tomato fan with a sprig of fresh parsley. Use to garnish individual servings or a large platter.

Sautéed Potato Cubes

Make a formal arrangement of crisp, golden potato cubes on casseroles, or sprinkle on salads.

FOR THE GARNISH
1 waxy potato, peeled
2 tablespoons sunflower oil
fresh sage leaves

1 Square off the sides of the potato. Cut it into ½-inch slices, then stack two or three slices together and cut into ½-inch cubes. Place in a colander, rinse under cold water, drain and pat dry on paper towels.

2 Heat the oil in a large frying pan. Add the potato cubes, turning to coat. Cook, tossing occasionally, for 10–15 minutes, until golden brown and tender. Drain briefly on paper towels. Arrange the cubes on the dish and finish the garnish with sage leaves.

COOK'S TIP: Sprinkle on mashed potatoes for a themed garnish.

Fluted Mushrooms

A traditional garnish for steak, these pretty mushrooms also go well with chops and grilled foods.

FOR THE GARNISH
4 large button mushrooms
1 tablespoon butter

1 Holding a mushroom by the stem, use a fine knife to cut a curved groove from the center of the cap to the edge.

2 Turning the mushroom slightly, make similar grooves, each following the line of the first. Trim the stem level with the base of the cap. Repeat with the remaining mushrooms. Melt the butter in a small frying pan and sauté the mushrooms on both sides until golden and tender.

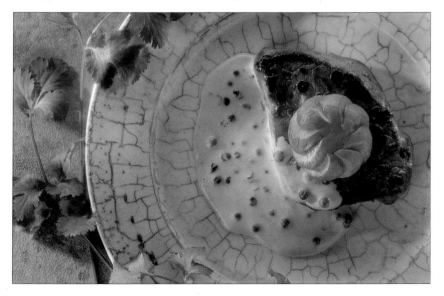

Cucumber Ribbons

These impressive loops of refreshing cucumber go especially well with rich roasts such as duck, game and pork.

FOR THE GARNISH
1 cucumber

1 Cut the cucumber into 2-inch lengths, then cut the pieces lengthwise into quarters. Make 6–7 fine horizontal cuts into the cucumber pieces, leaving ½ inch intact at one end.

2 Fold each slice over to form a loop, starting at the top and working down, until 5–6 loops have been made. Place on a serving platter, skin-side up.

COOK'S TIP: Cucumber ribbons, marinated in a little rice wine vinegar, then mixed with chopped parsley, make an interesting addition to a salad.

Cucumber Flower

This is a magnificent Chinese garnish and the perfect decoration for a tasty stir-fry.

FOR THE GARNISH
6-inch piece cucumber

1 Cut the cucumber in half lengthwise and remove the seeds. Place each half cut-side down, and cut at an angle into 3-inch lengths. Cut into fine slices, stopping ¼ inch short of the cut side, so that the slices remain attached.

2 Fan the slices out with the fingers. Turn in alternate slices to form loops. Bend the length into a semi-circle with the loops on the outside so that they resemble petals.

COOK'S TIP: Make the cucumber garnish when you are preparing the stir-fry ingredients.

Leek Haystacks

Stacks of golden leek look great with vegetable casseroles and fish.

FOR THE GARNISH
1 large leek
2 tablespoons all-purpose flour
oil, for deep-frying

1 Slice the leek lengthwise in half and then into quarters. Cut into 2-inch lengths and then into fine julienne strips. Place the strips in a bowl, sprinkle on the flour and toss well.

2 In a large saucepan, heat the oil to 325°F. Drop small spoonfuls of the floured leeks into the oil and cook for 30–45 seconds, until golden. Drain on paper towels. Repeat with the remaining leeks. Garnish the dish with small stacks of leeks.

Phyllo Stars

Light, crispy phyllo pastry stars make an unusual garnish for salads and casseroles.

FOR THE GARNISH
3 phyllo pastry sheets,
    thawed if frozen
1 tablespoon sunflower oil
1 teaspoon mild chili powder

1 Preheat the oven to 400°F. Carefully lay out a sheet of phyllo pastry. Brush lightly with oil and sprinkle one-third of the chili powder on it.

2 Place another sheet of phyllo pastry on top and dust with another third of chili powder. Repeat with the remaining sheet of phyllo pastry.

3 Using a large star cutter, stamp out stars from the layered phyllo. Transfer to a lightly oiled baking sheet and bake for 7–8 minutes, until golden and crisp.

4 Place a few stars close together on top of the food for an attractive effect.

Tomato Roses

An impressive garnish for a summer buffet table, these tomato roses require a steady hand. Add a sprig of basil, if desired.

FOR THE GARNISH
3 firm tomatoes

2 With the skin-side out and starting at the stem end, coil the peel loosely to within ¾ inch of the end. Set the coil upright so that it resembles a rosebud and tuck the end loosely underneath. Repeat with the remaining tomatoes.

1 Using a swivel-blade vegetable peeler and starting at the base of one of the tomatoes, peel it in one long, continuous strip. Work carefully and slowly to avoid breaking the strip, and keep the peel as thin as possible.

Tomato Suns

Bring a touch of summertime to fish, shellfish, kebabs and salads with these cherry tomato suns.

FOR THE GARNISH
2 ripe cherry tomatoes

2 Cut the quarters as before so that there are eight segments, joined at the base. Slide the top of the knife under the point of each segment and ease the skin off toward the base, stopping just short of it. Gently fold the segments back to mimic the sun's rays. Make another sun in the same way.

1 Place a tomato stem-side down and cut lightly into the skin across the top, edging the knife down toward the base on either side. Turn the tomato 90° and repeat.

Berry Garland

This stunning fruit and herb garland creates a bold and refreshingly scented border for scoops of ice cream or sorbet.

FOR THE GARNISH
1 bunch of mint
selection of berries, including
    red currants, strawberries, raspberries
    and blueberries

1 Place a large sprig of mint on the rim of a serving plate, then build up a garland using more sprigs.

2 With the leaves in place, link them with strings of red currants. Cut the strawberries in half. Arrange the strawberry halves on the garland, together with the other fruit. Place the fruits at different angles for a decorative effect.

Caramelized Citrus Zest

Add a tangy touch to tarts, molds and mousses with this delicious decoration attractively swirled into little nests.

FOR THE GARNISH
1 lemon
1 lime
1–2 tablespoons confectioners' sugar

1 Preheat the broiler. Using a swivel-blade vegetable peeler, remove the zest from the lemon and lime in long strips. Slice into fine julienne strips.

2 Place in a small saucepan of water, bring to a boil and simmer for 5 minutes. Drain, refresh under cold water and drain again. Pat dry with paper towels. Spread out the zest on a sheet of waxed paper.

3 Dredge the citrus zest with confectioners' sugar. Toss to coat, then transfer to a foil-lined broiler pan. Broil for 2–3 minutes, until the sugar just melts. Let cool and harden. Pile the citrus zest on the dessert and dust with confectioners' sugar before serving.

Frosted Petals

Sprinkle frosted rose petals on cookies, cakes and mousses. Whole roses can also be frosted in this way.

FOR THE GARNISH
1 rose
1 egg white
superfine sugar, for sprinkling

1 Separate the petals of the rose. Whisk the egg white until it starts to become foamy. Using a paint brush, gently brush egg white on each of the rose petals, covering them completely.

2 Sprinkle superfine sugar on a sheet of waxed paper. Place the rose petals on the sheet and sprinkle on more sugar, then toss lightly until completely covered. Place the rose petals on a wire rack and let sit for several hours, until completely dry.

VARIATION: Other suitable edible flowers include primroses, violets, pansies, borage, mallow and marigolds. Make sure the petals are pesticide-free, have no blemishes and have not been polluted with traffic fumes.

Meringue Crests

These melt-in-your-mouth meringues are a delightful decoration on filled crêpes, warm pies and tarts.

FOR THE GARNISH
1 egg white
¼ cup sugar

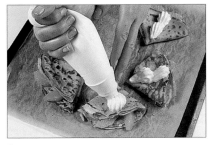

2 Arrange the crêpes on the prepared baking sheet and pipe the shells directly onto them. Bake for 5–6 minutes, until the meringue is golden.

1 Preheat the oven to 400°F. Line a baking sheet with nonstick baking parchment. Whisk the egg whites until soft peaks form. Gradually add the sugar, a spoonful at a time, whisking constantly, until stiff and glossy. Spoon into a piping bag fitted with a star nozzle.

VARIATION: For crisp meringues, pipe the meringue crests onto the prepared baking sheet. Dry out in an oven set to 300°F for 45 minutes. Cool. Use on cold desserts.

Chocolate Drizzles

Make random patterns or, if you have a steady hand, make special designs for trifles and mousses.

FOR THE GARNISH
4 ounces chocolate, broken
   into pieces

1 Line a baking sheet with nonstick baking parchment. Melt the chocolate in a heatproof bowl set over a pan of simmering water. Alternatively, melt in the microwave on medium power for 2 minutes.

2 Pour it into an icing bag fitted with a very small plain nozzle or a paper cone with the point snipped off. Drizzle the chocolate on the baking sheet in small, self-contained lattice shapes, such as circles or squares. Let set for about 30 minutes, until firm, then carefully peel off the paper.

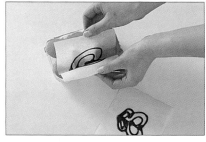

3 To make flowers, trace them onto the baking paper. Pipe chocolate on the design. For butterflies, trace the design onto small squares of baking paper and pipe on the chocolate. Leave until just beginning to set, then place the butterfly, still on the paper, in a box, such as an egg carton, so that it bends in the center. Chill until needed.

Chocolate Shapes

These are easy to prepare with melted chocolate and are ideal for decorating cakes or other desserts.

FOR THE GARNISH
4 ounces chocolate, broken
  into pieces

1 Line a baking sheet with nonstick baking parchment. Melt the chocolate in a heatproof bowl set over a pan of simmering water. Alternatively, melt in the microwave on medium power for 2 minutes.

2 Pour the chocolate onto the prepared baking sheet and spread evenly to a thickness of about ⅛ inch. Let cool for about 30 minutes, until firm.

3 Invert the chocolate onto another sheet of baking parchment and, using a sharp knife and a straight edge, trim the sides to make a perfect rectangle. Using the straight edge, mark even squares, rectangles or diamond shapes and cut with a knife.

Chocolate and Coconut Curls

This method makes quite large curls, which may be used separately on individual portions or together to decorate cakes and desserts.

FOR THE GARNISH
4 ounces chocolate, broken into pieces
piece of fresh coconut

1 Melt the chocolate in a heatproof bowl set over a pan of simmering water. Alternatively, melt in the microwave on medium power for 2 minutes. Spread the melted chocolate thinly and evenly on a cool, smooth surface. Set aside until it is just set.

2 Push a metal scraper or cheese slicer across the surface, at an angle of 25°, to remove thin shavings of chocolate, which will curl gently against the blade. If the chocolate sets too hard, it may be too brittle to curl and must be gently melted again. Use a swivel-blade vegetable peeler to shave thin strips off the side of the piece of coconut. Gently place the curls on the cake or dessert.

Chocolate-dipped Fruit

Chocolate-dipped cape gooseberries and strawberries are perfect partners for chocolate cakes and desserts.

FOR THE GARNISH
8 cape gooseberries
2 ounces semi-sweet chocolate pieces
8 strawberries

1 Line a baking sheet with nonstick baking parchment. Open the papery husks of the cape gooseberries and twist back to form a little umbrella.

2 Melt the chocolate in a heatproof bowl set over a pan of simmering water. Alternatively, melt in the microwave on medium power for 2 minutes. Holding each cape gooseberry by the husk, dip half the fruit in the melted chocolate. Transfer to the prepared baking sheet to set. Repeat the process with all the strawberries.

Broiled Pears and Stilton with a Gilded Pear

Gilding is a stunning way to finish a dish. Any fruit can be transformed like this and even used for a table decoration.

Makes 24

INGREDIENTS
4 large ripe pears
4 ounces Stilton cheese
2 tablespoons plain yogurt
salt and freshly ground
    black pepper

FOR THE GARNISH
1 small pear, preferably with the
    stalk intact
1 book of edible gold leaf

1 First, make the garnish. Stand the pear upright. If necessary, trim about ¼ inch off the base so that it remains level.

2 Very carefully tear off pieces of gold leaf and drape over the pear, smoothing and pressing the leaf on gently until the pear is covered completely and evenly. Set aside.

3 Preheat the broiler to high and line a broiler pan with aluminum foil. Cut the pears lengthwise into thick slices on either side of the cores. Using a small diamond-shape cutter, stamp out about 24 diamonds of pear, and place in the broiler pan.

4 Crumble the Stilton into a bowl. Stir in the yogurt to make a creamy paste and season to taste with salt and pepper. Place a teaspoonful of the mixture on each pear diamond. Broil until the Stilton starts to melt and bubble. Arrange on a platter with the gilded pear and serve immediately.

VARIATION: Gilded fruit is perfect for adding a finishing touch to special dishes, such as blinis with smoked salmon or caviar, or a tray of petits fours, which could include gilded berries.

Potato Blinis with Dill Cream and Smoked Salmon Roses

A rose of smoked fish complements fluffy potato blinis perfectly. The roses also look elegant on fish dishes, such as turbot and lobster.

Serves 8

INGREDIENTS

1 pound floury potatoes, peeled
  and quartered
¼ cup dill mustard
1¼ cups crème fraîche
3 eggs, beaten
¼ cup self-rising flour
⅔ cup heavy cream
2 egg whites
1 teaspoon grated nutmeg
oil, for frying
salt and freshly ground
  black pepper

FOR THE GARNISH
8 smoked salmon slices
sprigs of fresh dill

1 Cook the potatoes in lightly salted boiling water for 15 minutes, until tender. Drain, return to the pan and place over low heat to drive off any remaining moisture. Pass through a food mill or press through a strainer with a wooden spoon. Mash lightly, then cool, cover and chill. Mix the dill mustard and crème fraîche in a bowl, cover and set aside.

2 Whisk the eggs and flour into the chilled mashed potatoes. Bring the cream to a boil in a small saucepan, then whisk it into the potato mixture to make a batter. Whisk the egg whites until stiff peaks form, then gently fold into the potato batter. Season with nutmeg and salt and pepper to taste. Set aside.

3 To make the garnish, fold one slice of smoked salmon in half lengthwise. Holding one end with the finger and thumb, start winding the salmon around on itself to form a loose pinwheel, using the other hand.

4 Set the salmon rose on a work surface and pinch the bottom to hold it together. Using a toothpick or small knife, gently separate each layer to form petals. Use the remaining salmon to make more roses in the same way. Cover and chill.

5 Preheat the oven to 275°F. Line a baking sheet with waxed paper. Heat a little oil in a small nonstick frying pan or crêpe pan. Ladle in about ½ inch batter. Cook until golden and bubbles have started to form on the top. Flip over and cook the other side until golden.

6 Slide the blini onto the prepared baking sheet and keep warm in the oven, while you make seven more in the same way, adding more oil as needed. Serve the blinis warm, topping each one with a spoonful of the dill cream and a smoked salmon rose and adding an extra garnish of dill.

Apricot Ice Cream Under a Caramel Cage

Caramel is a favorite with confectioners because of its decorative possibilities. Here, a caramel cage covers homemade apricot ice cream.

Serves 6-8

INGREDIENTS
1 pound dried apricots
3¾ cups cold brewed
    Earl Grey tea
½ cup light brown sugar
2 tablespoons brandy or gin (optional)
1¼ cups whipping cream

FOR THE GARNISH
3 cups sugar
¾ cup water
½ cup liquid glucose
oil, for greasing

1 Place the apricots in a large bowl and add the tea. Cover and set aside to soak for 4 hours or overnight.

2 Transfer the apricots and the tea to a saucepan. Add the brown sugar and bring to a boil, stirring until it has dissolved. Simmer over low heat for 15–20 minutes, until the apricots are tender. Let cool.

VARIATION: Caramel cages can be used to decorate other desserts, such as floating island, cold soufflés, poached peaches and raspberries and cream.

3 Process the apricots and cooking liquid in a food processor or blender into a rough purée. Stir in the brandy or gin, if using.

4 Whip the cream until soft peaks form. Fold in the apricot purée, mixing well. Transfer to a freezer-proof container and freeze for 2 hours. Beat with an electric mixer until smooth, then return to the freezer for at least 8 hours. Alternatively, you can add the unwhipped cream to the dried apricot purée and place the mixture in an ice cream maker; churn, following the manufacturer's instructions.

5 To make the garnish, place the sugar and water in a small saucepan. Stir over low heat until the sugar dissolves. Bring to a boil and add the liquid glucose. Cook until the mixture is pale caramel. Cool slightly. Oil the back of a ladle.

6 Using a teaspoon, trail caramel on the ladle in horizontal and vertical lines until a cage is formed. Let harden, then gently ease off. Repeat with the remaining caramel, reheating if necessary, to make six to eight cages. To serve, arrange scoops of ice cream on individual dessert plates and place the caramel cages over the ice cream.

Lemon Mousse with Shortbread Hearts

Shortbread can be stamped out into any shape, baked and then lightly dusted with confectioners' sugar.

Serves 6–8

INGREDIENTS
4 sheets of gelatin
¼ cup water
1 cup mascarpone cheese
1 cup fromage frais
3 tablespoons confectioners' sugar, sifted
grated zest and juice of 2 lemons
3 egg whites

FOR THE GARNISH
¼ cup chopped
    almonds, toasted
6 tablespoons sugar
1¼ cups all-purpose flour
½ cup butter, diced
sifted confectioners' sugar, for dusting
frosted rose petals (optional)

1 Soak the gelatin in the water until soft. Beat the mascarpone, fromage frais and confectioners' sugar together until fluffy. Squeeze out the water from the gelatin and melt with the lemon juice in a small saucepan. Cool slightly, then beat into the mascarpone mixture.

VARIATION: Shortbread hearts would go well with a fruit parfait, sorbet, ice cream and, of course, coeurs à la crème.

2 Whisk the egg whites until stiff. Fold into the mascarpone mixture, together with half the lemon zest. Spoon into serving dishes and chill for 3–4 hours, until set.

3 Meanwhile, make the garnish. Process the almonds and sugar in a food processor until fine. Add the flour and mix. Add the butter and process until a dough forms. Turn out and knead lightly. Wrap in plastic wrap and chill for 20 minutes. Preheat the oven to 350°F. Line a baking sheet with nonstick baking parchment.

4 Roll out the dough on a lightly floured surface until ¼ inch thick. Stamp out heart-shaped cookies, transfer to the prepared baking sheet and bake for 10–12 minutes. Cool. Dust with confectioners' sugar. Top the mousse with the remaining lemon zest and serve with the shortbread hearts and frosted rose petals, if desired.

Chocolate Yule Log with Marzipan Decorations

Colorful marzipan holly leaves and berries, as well as toadstools, decorate this rich chocolate cake.

Makes 1 large log

INGREDIENTS
3 eggs
generous ⅓ cup sugar,
    plus extra for sprinkling
generous ½ cup self-rising flour
1 tablespoon unsweetened cocoa powder

FOR THE CHOCOLATE CREAM
generous ⅓ cup sugar
5 tablespoons water
3 egg yolks
¾ cup unsalted butter
3 ounces semi-sweet chocolate, melted

FOR THE GARNISH
3 ounces marzipan
green and red food coloring
confectioners' sugar and
    unsweetened cocoa powder for dusting

1 Preheat the oven to 375°F. Grease and line a 13 x 9-inch jelly roll pan. Whisk the eggs and sugar in a heatproof bowl set over a pan of simmering water until thick and pale. Remove the bowl from the heat and whisk until cool and the whisk leaves a trail on the surface. Fold in the flour and cocoa powder and pour into the prepared pan.

2 Bake for 18–20 minutes, until the cake springs back when lightly pressed.

3 Sprinkle a sheet of nonstick baking paper with sugar. Invert the cake onto the paper and peel off the lining paper. Trim off the edges and, starting from a short edge, roll up the cake and paper.

4 To make the chocolate cream, dissolve the sugar in the water in a pan set over low heat, then boil rapidly until it reaches 225°F on a candy thermometer. Alternatively, test by dipping two cold spoons in the syrup. If threads form as the spoons are separated, it is ready.

5 Whisk the syrup into the egg yolks in a bowl until thick and pale. Cool. Beat the butter until light and fluffy, then beat the egg mixture into the butter until thick. Fold in the chocolate.

6 Unroll the cake, discarding the paper. Spread with half the chocolate cream and re-roll. Spread the outside with the remaining chocolate cream and mark the surface to make it look like bark. Chill until set.

7 Color one-third of the marzipan green and a tiny piece red. Make holly and ivy leaves from the green marzipan, marking veins with a knife. Make berries from the red.

8 Shape toadstool caps from balls of uncolored marzipan and attach to short, rolled stems. Dust with cocoa powder. Arrange the decorations on the log and dust with confectioners' sugar.

Carrot Cake with Marzipan Carrots

An amusing touch, the little marzipan carrots make this cake special.

Serves 8

INGREDIENTS
generous 1 cup sugar
3 eggs
scant 1 cup vegetable oil
grated zest and juice of 1 orange
2 cups self-rising
   whole-wheat flour
1 teaspoon ground cinnamon
½ teaspoon freshly grated nutmeg
½ teaspoon salt
2½ cups grated carrot,
   squeezed dry
1 cup walnuts, ground

FOR THE ICING
1 cup cream cheese
2 tablespoons honey
1 tablespoon orange juice

FOR THE GARNISH
2 ounces marzipan
orange food coloring
angelica
2 walnut halves, optional

1 Preheat the oven to 350°F. Grease and line the bottom of an 8-inch round cake pan. Beat the sugar, eggs, oil, orange zest and juice together until light and frothy. Sift in the flour, spices and salt and beat for another minute.

2 Stir in the carrot and nuts and transfer to the prepared pan. Bake for 1½–1¾ hours, until risen and a skewer inserted into the cake comes out clean. Cool in the pan for 10 minutes, then transfer to a wire rack to cool completely.

3 To make the icing, beat the cheese, honey and orange juice together until smooth. Chill for 30 minutes.

4 To make the carrots, tint the marzipan orange, kneading the color in well. Break off small pieces and roll between the palms of the hands to form carrot shapes.

5 Using a small knife, press marks around the sides and stick a small piece of angelica in the top of each. Remove the icing from the refrigerator and spread it on top of the cooled cake. Arrange the carrots in a bunch in the center of the cake and decorate with walnut halves, if using.

Rich Chocolate Leaf Gâteau

This elegantly decorated and utterly delicious chocolate cake would make a superb dinner-party dessert.

Serves 8

INGREDIENTS
3 ounces semi-sweet chocolate,
    broken into squares
⅔ cup milk
¾ cup unsalted butter, softened
1⅓ cups light brown sugar
3 eggs
2¼ cups all-purpose flour
2 teaspoons baking powder
5 tablespoons light cream

FOR THE FILLING AND TOPPING
8 ounces semi-sweet chocolate,
    broken into squares
1 cup heavy cream
¼ cup raspberry jam

FOR THE GARNISH
fresh rose leaves with well-defined veins
2 ounces semi-sweet chocolate,
    broken into squares
2 ounces white chocolate,
    broken into squares

1 First, make the chocolate leaves. Wash the leaves and pat thoroughly dry on paper towels. Melt the semi-sweet and white chocolate in separate heatproof bowls set over simmering water. Alternatively, melt the semi-sweet chocolate in the microwave on medium power for 2 minutes and the white chocolate on low power for 2 minutes.

2 Line a baking sheet with waxed paper. Using a medium-size paintbrush, thickly coat the underside of each leaf with melted chocolate, taking care not to paint over the edge of the leaves or the leaf will not peel off the chocolate. Place the leaves, chocolate side facing up, on the paper and let set in a cool place.

3 To make the cake, preheat the oven to 375°F. Grease and line the bottoms of two 8½-inch cake pans. Melt the chocolate with the milk over low heat, then let the mixture cool slightly.

4 Cream the butter with the sugar until light and fluffy. Beat in the eggs, one at a time. Sift the flour and baking powder onto the mixture and gently fold in. Stir in the chocolate mixture and the cream, mixing until smooth. Divide the mixture among the prepared pans and smooth the surface.

5 Bake for 30–35 minutes or until well risen and firm to the touch. Cool in the pans for a few minutes, then turn out onto wire racks to cool completely.

6 Meanwhile, to make the topping, heat the chocolate and cream in a small saucepan over low heat, stirring frequently until the chocolate has melted. Pour into a bowl and let cool, then whisk until the mixture begins to hold its shape.

7 Sandwich the cooled cake layers together with raspberry jam. Spread the chocolate topping on the cake and swirl with a knife. Place the cake on a serving plate. Carefully peel the real leaves off the chocolate ones. Decorate the cake with the chocolate leaves.

This edition is published by Southwater

Southwater is an imprint of
Anness Publishing Limited
Hermes House
88–89 Blackfriars Road
London SE1 8HA
tel. 020 7401 2077
fax. 020 7633 9499

Distributed in the USA by
Anness Publishing Inc.
27 West 20th Street
Suite 504
New York, NY 10011
tel. (212) 807 6739
fax. (212) 807 6813

Distributed in the UK by
The Manning Partnership,
251–253 London Road East, Batheaston,
Bath BA1 7RL, UK
tel. (0044) 01225 852 727
fax. (0044) 01225 852 852

Distributed in Australia by
Sandstone Publishing,
Unit 1, 360 Norton Street, Leichhardt,
New South Wales 2040, Australia
tel. (0061) 2 9560 7888
fax. (0061) 2 9560 7488

Southwater is an imprint of Anness Publishing Limited

© 2000 Anness Publishing Limited

Publisher: Joanna Lorenz
Editor: Valerie Ferguson
Series Designer: Bobbie Colgate Stone
Designer: Andrew Heath
Editorial Reader: Marion Wilson
Production Controller: Joanna King

Recipes contributed by: Janet Brinkworth,
Kathy Brown, Nicola Diggins, Christine France, Carole Handslip,
Bridget Jones, Kathy Mann, Sarah Maxwell, Janice Murfitt, Angela Nilsen,
Louise Pickford, Elizabeth Wolf-Cohen.

Photography: William Adams-Lingwood, Karl Adamson, Edward Allwright,
David Armstrong, Steve Baxter, James Duncan, Michelle Garrett, Amanda Heywood,
Tim Hill, Don Last.

1 3 5 7 9 10 8 6 4 2